WordPress
The Complete Beginner's Guide to Mastery.
A Closer Look At Using One of the World's Top Website Creation Platforms

Table of Contents

Introduction

WordPress is a very popular option for you to consider when you are aiming to get the most out of your online blogging plans. You can create a great blog by using the WordPress system thanks to how easy it is to use.

Better yet, you can create an entire website with WordPress. Every individual page on your site can be adjusted in a variety of ways.

This guide will help you learn about how to use WordPress to create your own website or blog. You will learn about how to get access to WordPress and how to use its many features. Details on how to prepare posts and make your content more interactive are also included in this guide.

You will also learn about how to work with plugins and how to let people interact with you. Information on how to organize a site properly and how to many it look visually appealing will also be included here.

The points listed here can be used for any type of WordPress site. Some of these ideas might actually be perfect for your site if you're trying to start an online business while using WordPress as the backbone to getting your site ready. The functionality of WordPress and its ability to protect your information will certainly make a real difference in terms of what you're getting out of it.

The information listed here will be essential for when you are looking to take that next step in creating a quality website or blog. You might be surprised at what you will get out of WordPress when you use it the right way.

Chapter 1 – What Is WordPress?

To successfully use WordPress, you have to be aware of what makes WordPress such an efficient option for your website or blog creation needs. WordPress is an open-source CMS, or Content Management System, program that you can utilize right now to create a great website.

WordPress is a program that is installed onto a web server. It can be accessed through your own computer as you can log into a WordPress account. You just have to get onto the website you are looking to edit and then access to WordPress portal.

The simplicity of WordPress and its ease of use have made it to where there are more than 60 million sites around the world that use WordPress as a blog or website creation tool. The odds are you'll find it to be useful for your site just as well.

Why Use WordPress?

WordPress has become a trusted name in the field of website creation thanks to many assorted benefits:

- This is a very easy to use solution. You don't even need to edit HTML to make it work.

- You can manage your page from any computer so long as you have access to a WordPress account.

- You can add keywords, descriptions and other pieces of meta information onto your WordPress page.

- Your site is especially scalable in that you can add new pages onto your site as necessary.

- Various additional plug-ns can be added onto your site to make it more functional.

- Multiple people can help you out with your WordPress site. You can create many login accounts for access to your WordPress page.

WordPress will certainly work wonders for your website or blog creation demands. However, you need to get it installed properly if it is going to be of any use to you. This is where the next chapter comes into play.

Chapter 2 – How To Get Access to WordPress

To get your own blog or website created with WordPress, you have to first get access to it. The installation process is amazingly easy to manage.

Getting Access To WordPress

You can find WordPress from its official website at wordpress.com. However, you must ensure that you can run WordPress.

A proper web host is needed. You can be the host but you can always rely upon another hosting server to help you out.

The host must have PHP version 5.6 or higher and either MySQL 5.6 or MariaDB 10.0 or higher. These should all be easy to support through many servers.

You can always get the newest edition of the WordPress program from wordpress.com but you might need to ask your host for help in the event that you need it. You should ask your host if your account can support WordPress.

This should be supported by most computers and should be easy to use. Make sure you check on whether or not you can make it work before you start to use it though.

Installing WordPress

After you download the latest edition of
WordPress from wordpress.com, you need to
use a few steps for installing it.
The newest edition of WordPress should be
available on the main site. Stick with the newest
version so you will be fully protected with the
latest quality features.

1. After downloading the file, unzip the
   package. This should contain the files for
   running WordPress.

2. Create a database for WordPress use on
   your server. A proper database user for
   MySQL or MariaDB should also be
   created. The user must have full
   privileges to access and edit data on
   WordPress.

3. Upload the files from the WordPress
   download to your web server. The files
   should be moved to the root directory on
   your server.

4. Run the installation script by entering in
   your URL in a web browser. The URL
   should be the one that the files were
   uploaded to.

What About Auto-Installers?

As fast as the installation process might be, you can always use an auto-installer to help you get ready. An auto-installer will take care of many of the technical aspects of getting WordPress ready for your site. Programs like APS, Fantastico and Installatron can help you with the installation process.

To get any of these programs to work, you will have to send in information on your FTP and database. You must be as specific as possible when using such a program so you will have enough information available for people to use. The installation process will vary based on the auto-installer that you use. Also, it typically costs extra for you to use an auto-installer, what with such a program being used to simplify the process of getting WordPress ready for your use.

Creating a WordPress Account

After you have installed WordPress onto your server or host, you can establish your own account. You will particularly have to choose a domain to make it all work out right.

It is free to get a web address with a WordPress extension. For instance, if you were to create a website about vacuum cleaners, you can use the domain vacuumreport.wordpress.com for free.

It will cost extra to get a domain without the WordPress name on it. You will have to pay money with either WordPress or with a separate registrar to get vacuumreport.com ready for your use.

You must also determine which membership tier you want to sign up with. Information on the membership tiers used by WordPress are listed in the next section.

After you finalize information on the domain you want to work with, you have to send in your email address and username information. A password must also be sent in as needed so you can access your page.

Three Tiers of Membership

There are three particular membership tiers for you to watch for when getting on WordPress:

1. The Free tier provides you with a free page and up to 3 GB of space.

2. The Premium option is for $8.25 per month and is billed on an annual basis. This gives you 13 GB in space, a custom design setup, no ads on your page and your own custom site address.

3. The Business tier is for $24.92 per month and is also billed annually. This provides

you with unlimited space and access to Google Analytics data.

Think about the use you have for your WordPress site before choosing an option. You can always stick with the Business option if you plan on selling things on your WordPress site. Still, you have to think about your commitment to your site when planning it and making your data ready.

Be careful when getting WordPress set up properly. You have to make sure you install it right and that you get a proper account working on it.

Chapter 3 – The Main Dashboard

After you log into your WordPress account with your appropriate user ID and password, you should get access to an appropriate dashboard. This will help you with getting your page updated.

You can access the dashboard by adding /wp-admin onto the end of your WordPress URL. It should prompt you to log in if you haven't done so already.

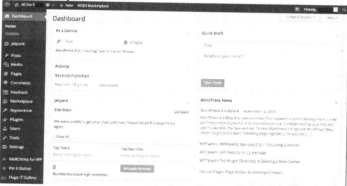

The dashboard will include information on the following:

- Any new updates to your page

- Information on the version of WordPress you are using and the theme you have for it

- Details on what is new with WordPress

- Information on how many people are visiting your page

- A quick draft section that lets you quickly draft new posts that you can edit or upload later on

- Reports on any comments you might be getting from other people

- Additional information depending on the particular plugins you have installed; the picture you just saw has the Akismet plugin installed and shows details on how it has blocked some dangerous login attempts, for example

What Is Quick Draft?

Quick Draft is a feature where you can quickly create content for use on your page. This works with two basic sections. It has a title section and a box for you to enter the post into.
You can enter in a title for a post and then type in that post into the appropriate box right underneath it. When you are done, click the Save Draft button.

This allows you to save information that you might think of as you see fit. You can quickly enter in that data into your WordPress account and then access it later on for when you want to update or refine that information and get it posted onto your page.

Quick Draft is perfect for when you have great ideas that you want to add to your WordPress site and you want to save them for later use. The data can be accessed through the Posts section later on so you can expand upon that information and eventually upload it.

Many Sections Are Accessible

There are various different sections that are found on the left-hand side of your dashboard. These sections include ones that let you adjust what is on your WordPress page.

The sections that you can include should entail the following:

- There should be a posts section that lets you take a look at individual posts you have created.

- A pages section will lead you to information on individual pages you've created. This includes pages where separate posts will head to.

- A media page will help you adjust the media files that you might add. These include any videos or photos that you want to edit or post online.

- A separate section dedicated to plugins is also there. This lists details on the plugins you have installed and what is active. Added details on plugins will be discussed later in this guide.

The dashboard should provide you with access to all the parts of your WordPress site. It will inform you on what is going on with your site and help you get the most out of the site you are trying to establish.

Chapter 4 – Establishing a Theme

To make your page stand out, you need to create a good theme. A theme refers to the particular physical arrangement of your site or blog. It can entail a good color scheme or a series of boxes where data can be organized.

A great theme is a necessity as it does more than just make your page look appealing. It also helps you figure out how your data is to be arranged. It lets you know where your content will be seen and how easy it will be for people to read your work.

WordPress proudly offers a variety of theme templates for you to look for. These include themes with different color schemes and various boxes that you can add information onto. You can always create your own specific theme if you prefer.

Access the Appearance Section

To create a theme, you need to access the Appearance section on the dashboard. You can then browser through the various themes that are available through WordPress.

WordPress has a variety of featured themes for you to choose from. These can be adjusted as you see fit. You can also choose to create your own custom theme.

Adding Filters

As you look for a theme to use, you can always apply a series of filters onto your search. WordPress has a variety of filters to help you find a very specific theme that is right for your site.
The many filters for your use include the following options:

- The main color you want to use

- The layout of your theme; this includes layouts based on the number of columns you have or where sidebars are to be placed

- Filters based on the individual features of a page like a need to focus on particular images

After you find a template that meets your demands based on those filters, you can always preview that template and then install it. WordPress will automatically download and install the template. You can then choose to active it through the appropriate link that WordPress will lead you to.

Creating a Custom Theme

A great idea for making your WordPress page stand out is to create a custom theme. You can take the theme that you are using right now and adjust it in many ways to make it unique and special.

To do this, go to the Themes section of the Appearance part of your site and look for the active theme you are using. Click on the Customize button.

You will then have access to all the individual items that you can alter. As you customize the page, you will notice a full preview of your page on the right-hand side of the screen. This lets you adjust the page to your personal liking.

To start, you can alter the site title and tagline. These are the main descriptors of your site in terms of what your users can expect to see. Make sure this part of your page counts and that you use something descriptive, accurate and appealing.

The colors can also be adjusted around the theme. These should be altered to appropriate colors based on the content you are posting and the type of atmosphere you want to create.

Creating a Static Page

A static page can also be added if you need it. This can be added while you are customizing your theme in the Appearance part of the site. A static page is a traditional page that people will be led to as they visit your site. The default page on your WordPress page will typically feature the latest posts that you have added. However, you can choose to create a static page to create an introduction to your site. The static page will include any bits of information you might want to post to your page and let other people read.

Your readers will still be able to access your latest posts through individual sections on your WordPress page. They can always go to a section where information on the newest posts are listed as well. The static page simply creates a new spot that invites people to take a closer look at what you are offering.

Tips For a Good Theme

You must think about a few pointers as you are looking to get a great theme added to your WordPress page.

- Choose a layout that you know is good enough for most parts of your page. You need to try and keep the layout as consistent as possible around your entire site so readers won't be confused over how it is organized.

- Think about how images are to be used. Consider adding featured images that might be placed on the front page.

- Keep all updates on your page as visible as possible. A theme that includes an update section that lists information on the newest posts on one side or the screen should be perfect.

- Think about the content that you will post on your page and see if it's appropriate for a certain theme. That is, your content should be organized to where you've got enough words to work with on a certain spot without creating too much empty space.

Check carefully to see that you're creating a great theme for your WordPress site. You have to establish a sensible theme that is appealing and great for your use.

Chapter 5 – Preparing Posts

The posts that you put on your WordPress page will make the meat of your site or blog. These will feature the words, videos, pictures and other things that you want to convey to your readers.

You must create a good post and set up a series of categories for all of those posts. It's especially important to watch for how you're going to get your posts set up and made to be more unique and attractive to your readers.

Fortunately, WordPress has an arrangement that is very easy to use. You can simply go onto your WordPress client and then to the Posts section to create new posts that will be easy to add.

The Basics of Adding a Post

As you get onto WordPress, you will have to go to the Posts section of your module. Go to the Add New section to then establish a new post.

There are several steps to use at this particular point:

1. Enter in the title to your post.

2. Enter the content that you want to highlight in your post onto the appropriate spot. The editor program works like a traditional word processing program in that you can adjust the text based on its alignment, how content is being highlighted and so forth.

3. Use the Add Media button if you have a need to add any pictures, videos or other media content. This part will be addressed in a moment.

4. Click the Save Draft button if you plan on posting this later on.

5. If you are ready to post your content now, click the Publish button. There's also a section near the button that lets you schedule precisely when your content will be officially uploaded.

The process associated with creating a post is very easy to handle. However, there are many added things to consider when creating your post.

Adding Media

The Add Media button will provide you with the ability to insert many forms of media into your post. You can choose to insert many different pictures or video links to your site if necessary.

To do this, you have to use a few steps:

1. Go to the Upload Files section and choose a particular media file that you want to add to your post.

2. There's also the option to insert something from a URL address. This is for when you have a picture that is already online and you want to add it to your WordPress post.

3. The file you selected should be added to your media library. This is so you can edit your work later or post it on multiple pages if needed.

4. You can use the Edit Image link to adjust your content based on its size, its description and much more.

5. A title for the image or video can also be added. This is for when you need to create a descriptor that explains what the content is about.

6. A caption may be added if desired. This caption will appear at the bottom part of your media within your post.

7. The alignment of the image should then be adjusted. You can align this to appear on one side of the page. You can always use the post editor to adjust where the image will appear later on.

8. The size of the image can also be adjusted. You can create a smaller square thumbnail or you can opt to let it appear exactly as it originally was formatted. Be careful with the size of the image in

proportion with other images or content on your page.

9. The image or video should now be in your post.

This is an impressive feature but you might want to preview your post with your media in mind to ensure that your content will look great before you publish it. The Preview button will help you see what your content will look like as it goes live. This lets you figure out if you want to stick with a particular format or if it needs to be changed in any manner.

Creating Categories

The odds are you might be posting many different things onto your WordPress page with the intention of highlighting a vast wealth of knowledge. Creating a series of categories will be perfect for this occasion.
Your posts may be organized into a series of categories. These can be sorted through as simple tags that divide posts up based on what they are about.

The individual categories you create can also be highlighted on a margin or column on your page. Users can click on any of the categories to see only posts that are relevant to that particular category. This is important if you have a website that has loads of posts and you need to keep them organized.

There are a few steps to use when creating categories:

1. Go to the Posts section of the dashboard and click on the Categories subhead.

2. Enter in the name of a category that you want to create. Be advised that this will be visible on your site.

3. Create a slug for the category. This is the URL-friendly version of your name and will be used on your URL to differentiate your post from others.

4. A sub-category may also be created by choosing a parent category.

5. The categories should then be listed on the right-hand side of your post creation section.

Choose your categories based on what you know you will be posting. Think about how your content can be divided up into a variety of sections. This can help you see that you're getting your content up and running quite well. More importantly, it helps you keep your content organized as you add new things onto your site.

Adding Tags

You can also add tags to your individual posts. Tags are the keywords that will link up to your posts. These are used for search engine purposes to make your work more visible.
To create tags, you should go to the tag section on the right-hand side of your post generation menu. Enter in a series of keywords based on the content you are trying to upload. Make sure you add a comma in between each one so the computer will identify what is being used here.

The tags will appear around the bottom of your post as it is published. A user can click on one of these tags to find posts that are relevant to that particular tag. That is, they are posts that have that tag attached to them. Think of this as a smaller category based on a keyword.

Over time WordPress will keep a tally of the most used tags on your blog or website. It can even give you recommendations on what tags you should add based on the content you are posting.

There are no limits as to how many tags you can create or how many may be used on a post. Just be sure that the tags used on a post are organized properly enough.

Accessing Posts Later?

You can access your posts later on by clicking on the Add Posts section of the menu. This will list information on all the individual posts you've added. These can be browsed through based on points like their categories, who created the content and so forth.

This is especially important if you need to upload or edit your content over time. You have to make sure the content you hold is appropriately edited so it will look its best.

Remember that the posts you add onto your WordPress page will make a real difference in terms of what you are trying to share with other people who read your page. Make sure when creating an effective WordPress page that you are doing so with the right forms of content as needed.

Chapter 6 – Adding Pages

Static pages that will not include updated posts may be added to your WordPress site. Static pages will be perfect for when you need to add pages that describe certain products, services or ideas that you want to share.

The process of adding a page is very easy to use. You should use this process if you plan on adding information that is unique in some way but don't have a plan to update it in some manner.

This is particularly for pages that entail many bits of content including:

- About Us pages

- FAQ pages

- Pages that list instructions on products or services you have

- Pages describing items you might have for sale

- Schedule pages that list information on upcoming events you might be holding

There are many steps associated with adding a page but it's very easy to go through them all.

1. Go to the Pages section on the dashboard and select a new option.

2. Add a title to your page.

3. Add the content to that page. The space should be similar to what it looks like when you're creating a traditional post.

4. Click the Publish button if you are ready to post your page.

In terms of creating links to your page, you can always ask to get them added to specific sections of the page like the top or bottom margins. For instance, a link to your About Us page may be added to a margin. This should link to the appropriate URL for the page that you created. You can also choose to create a parent page with a template. This entails a few added steps to make it work.

1. As you prepare your page, go to the parent page section on the right hand side of the screen.

2. Click on the particular page that you want your new page to be associated with. In most cases your home page will be linked to it. You can get an About Us page to be listed as a child page to the home one, for instance.

3. Select the order in which the page will appear. An About Us page can be listed at the first one to see off of the main page.

This is perfect to use but be advised that the URL structure of some pages might be impacted based on what the parent page is and what child pages come after it.

The option to create pages for your WordPress site should be used if you plan on having a website with static content on it. Make sure the static content is organized properly and that you have the right parent pages set up to separate everything.

Chapter 7 – Encouraging Interactivity

You need to let your readers have a say when it comes to making your WordPress site work well. There are many reasons why it's important for them to have a voice:

- You need to show your readers that you are invested in whatever it is they want to say.

- You need to hear more about what you are doing right or wrong as you are preparing your site.

- You can even collect information from people who want to learn more about your work. This could be perfect if you're planning on selling things on your WordPress site.

It is a great idea to encourage a sense of interactivity with others on your WordPress page. That is, you can have people do one of many things while staying in touch with you. You can get people to send their email addresses or other bits of information to you. This can help you get new leads as you will have the ability to send updates to them about whatever your site is about. These include automatic messages for when you update your site.

You can also add social media buttons that allow people to share your site with others on various social media pages. This is perfect in today's connected world.

Also, there is the option to let people comment on your pages. This is perfect for when they might have new ideas or thoughts that need to be added to your site for whatever reason.

Support for Comments

The use of comments on your WordPress page is an important point to see. You don't always have to use comments on your page but it helps to at least let your readers have a say.

Comments are typically enabled on your posts and pages by default. You can choose to disable comments on individual spots if desired.

You can adjust how comments appear on your page by going to the Settings section off your dashboard and then choosing the Discussion menu. You can choose to allow your site to automatically accept comments if desired.

There's always the option to choose individual pages that you might want to have comments on and what you don't want to put comments on. This is important if you have some pages or posts that might contain sensitive information that you want to keep people from discussing for whatever information.

There are a few additional controls to consider:

- You can always allow avatars to be displayed. People who have avatars through the Gravatar system can have their images linked to their accounts become visible.

- You can also choose to allow comments to be available at certain times. That is, a topic can be closed off after a certain period of time. This is ideal for cases where information might be time sensitive.

- A moderation option is also available on the Discussion menu. This allows you to approve individual comments that people send in before they go online. You can choose to approve comments and allow them to go live to ensure that anything unrelated to your topic is avoided. This is for cases where you don't expect to get far too many comments at a time.

Remember that allowing comments on your WordPress page can make a difference when you're trying to make your content interactive.

Preventing Spam

Sometimes people might abuse the comment sections on your WordPress site and post spam messages. These include advertisements for different things that people want to hawk. This keeps legitimate comments from being visible or even taken seriously.

The best thing you can do to prevent spam from getting into your comments is to use Akismet. This outside program is ideal for use in that it identifies spam messages and blocks IP addresses and usernames of known spammers. You need to use this program to protect your WordPress page because WordPress itself does not have any particular internal systems to do this for you. Having an outside system on hand is like adding a strong antivirus program to your computer. It keeps your setup secure and protected against many threats that could compromise your data.

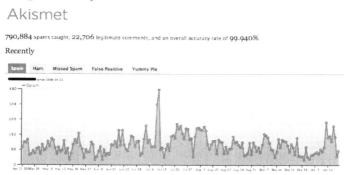

You can use Akismet by using a few steps.

1. Visit the Akismet website at akismet.com and choose a particular option for use.

A free version of Akismet will provide you with up to 50,000 checks each month. There are also advanced versions of the program that cost extra each month and are for business sites in particular. These advanced options offer more monthly checks, priority chat support, advanced statistics and even backup options in some cases. A more advanced paid option is better suited to those who have business pages to run and are trying to earn money. A free option should be good enough if you are just running a casual page and you're not trying to collect sensitive bits of data from people.

2. Install the Akismet module onto your WordPress page.

Information on how to install plugins will be discussed in the next chapter.

3. The plugin, when activated, will ask you to log into your Akismet account. An API key that has been provided to you by Akismet should then be entered in to confirm your account identity.

4. The program should then filter out spam posts and monitor what is happening on your site. It can also identify cases where

someone might try to break into your site by logging in under some kind of name.

5. Any spam posts that it does collect will be moved into a spam folder so you can see if any legitimate messages have accidentally gotten into your spam folder.

There are often times when real messages might get into your spam folder. Sometimes it's from a legitimate person who sends multiple pieces of information to you in a short span of time. Fortunately, Akismet is very accurate and should identify posts with care.
This outside plugin should be your best bet for keeping spam posts from being a threat.

Social Media Integration

Another option for allowing people to interact with your WordPress site is to add social media support. In particular, you can add new plugins that let people share your content on social media sites.
There are far too many social media integration programs to mention but here's a sampling of what you can find:

- Share This supports more than 120 different social networks.

- Floating Social creates a floating sharing bar that lets people share content on many major social media sites. The bar is very easy to see.

- Social Sharing by Danny is only 600 bytes in size as it adds a slim yet easy to view social media integration bar on your page.

- Social Icons has a series of small icons that can be added to your page. This can be customized to showcase one of more than 30 social networks.

The best part of these plugins is that a majority of them can be found on the WordPress website. WordPress lists details on all sorts of plug-ins on its website so you can get access to assorted plugs that are right for your use.

You should be careful when getting this part of your plan up and running though. Think about the types of social media accounts you're going to want to let people share your data on when choosing a social media integration program.

Take In Emails

You can always use WordPress to take in emails from other people. This is for cases where you need to get leads in terms of who might do business with you. This is ideal for when you are trying to sell things to people and you want your site to become more popular.

You can also use these email addresses with any autoresponder software program or other email program you have to use. You can use separate software programs to send email alerts to people about updates to your WordPress site among other things.

To take in emails, you must download a separate plugin to make it work. After this is done, you can install that plugin and look for the appropriate integration box on that plugin. This will let you install a new email box that will direct new email information to a database or other account of your choosing.

This can certainly do well for when you want to find people who want to show that they are interested in you. People who are interested in your work will certainly be willing to send their email addresses to you so you will consistently get plenty of new information on what's going on with your page.

Remember when creating your WordPress page that being in touch with other people can make a difference. Make sure you use the interactivity features listed here to make your content stand out.

Chapter 8 – Adding Plugins

You might be surprised at the immense variety of different plugins that you can use when getting WordPress to work for you. These plugins will add to the functionality of your page.

WordPress is an open source program, thus allowing people to create all sorts of plugins. There's no limit as to what people can do with these particular plugins.

In fact, WordPress directly promotes all sorts of plugins for use. By visiting the WordPress website, you can go to the Plugins section to find information on the hottest new plugins.

Best of all, a vast majority of plugins are free to use. Some options might require you to pay something extra to get access to some advanced features so be sure to check on what makes each individual page different from one another.

Let's take a closer look at the process associated with adding plugins to your WordPress site. It's not as hard to manage as you might think it could be.

What Can Plugins Be Used For?

Plugins can work for a variety of purposes:

- Some plugins allow you to add media files of all sorts with ease.

- Others allow you to integrate your work with social media pages.

- Some proofreading or reviewing plugins may be added. These include options that help you see if your grammar and syntax are correct.

- Others will allow you to copy information or update items based on what your database might show among other points.

- A shopping cart plugin can also be used if you want to make it easier for people to buy things on your site. A shopping cart allows people to share and send financial information in a secure environment so you can be paid when you sell people things and send them out.

WordPress is always getting new plugins from its extensive library of developers. Check around to see what new options are available for your use as you see fit.

How to Install a Plugin

Installing a plugin is as easy as installing a typical software program onto your computer. You'll have to see that your plugins are actually be read by WordPress before they can get to work.

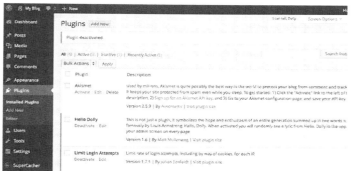

There are many steps associated with installing a plugin to use:

1. Download the proper package file for a plugin. You should be able to do this through the WordPress website depending on the plugin you want.

2. Move the files from the package file into the wp-content/plugins directory on your site.

3. Go to the Plugins section of your WordPress account and check to see if the plugin you have is up there. If not, go to the Add New section.

4. Choose the proper package file that has the plugin you have and click on the Install Now button.

5. Click the Activate button on the plugin you want to install. The program should automatically be installed and ready to use.

This basic process should work for most plugins. Check with the documentation for whatever plugin you want to add to see if yours is ready. The menu that shows the plugins you're using should include details on what is active, what a plugin does and a link to your particular plugin's website.

How to Uninstall a Plugin

The process for uninstalling a plugin is easy to do. You'll have to remove the directory for the plugin that has to be uninstalled. This can be done manually and will automatically deactivate the plugin.

Tips For Using Plugins

While the plugins you add to your site will certainly stand out and make it functional, there are a few additional considerations worth taking a look into as you're trying to get them ready. Here are some tips for using plugins that you need to review:

- Check on the website of whoever has developed a plugin before installing it. While the WordPress website has plenty of information on what plugins are about, the official sites for each one should be even more thorough.

- Make sure you update each plugin regularly. Newer versions will not only have more features but will also be a little more stable.

- Check and see if the plugins you want to use actually have some kind of value to your site. Don't download and install plugins that might not actually be necessary for whatever purpose you might hold.

- Think about how much data is used by each plugin. Some options might only contain a few bytes of data while others are more extensive.

- Look at the added functions that will appear on your dashboard. See that you can easily identify what your plugin adds to your dashboard or control system and that you know how to adjust those plugins as necessary.

Always be on the lookout for new plugins for your WordPress site. You might be surprised at how they can add more to your page.

Chapter 9 – Managing Users

Do you have multiple people who might be capable of adjusting things on your WordPress site? If so, you need to manage your users properly. You have to not only add new users when the time is right but also keep their permissions under control so they don't try to access more things than what they should be allowed to handle.

Individual roles and permissions are used as a means of allowing people to have access to various particular functions on your WordPress page. That is, people can add content but they cannot adjust the template or other features of a page in some cases.

Four Key Roles

There are four important roles that your users can handle when on WordPress:

1. The Administrator can add, edit and do anything on a WordPress page.

2. An Editor can edit, publish and remove posts or pages. The Editor can also manage all links, tags, comments and categories as needed.

3. An Author can create, edit, publish and delete posts. Authors can also upload videos or images for use on those posts.

4. A Contributor can edit posts. The Administrator will have to review the edits the Contributor makes before they can go live.

On a related note, you might come across a Subscriber role. This is for those who have registered and logged into a site to leave comments. Subscribers can leave comments on WordPress pages and posts but they cannot add or do anything else.

Adding a User

To add a user, you must follow these steps:
1. Go to the Users section of your WordPress dashboard.

2. Choose the Add New option.

3. Enter in information based on the user's name and the password.

4. Choose the particular role out of the four that the user will hold. A drop-down space will let you choose the particular role one has.

5. Send information on the login data to the user by email. You have the option to send it by email through WordPress.

Information on all your users should be listed right on the Users page. Check the All Users section to see who has access to your site. You also have the right to adjust the name of the user in terms of how it will appear. This is perfect for when a person's proper name is to appear in terms of being listed as the author of a page.

Changing Roles

You can also change someone's role on WordPress if you want to give a person more or fewer rules to work with. For instance, a person who edits posts could become capable of authoring totally new ones.

Here are some steps to use when changing a person's role:

1. Click on the particular user that you want to change a role for.

2. Select the Change Role To box and choose the particular role that you want a user to follow.

3. Click on the Change button. The user's role should be adjusted at this point.

Deleting Users

You can always delete users in the event that you don't need their services and you don't want them to access your WordPress page to edit things again.
The steps to use are as follows:

1. Click on the user that needs to be removed.

2. Choose the Delete action from the drop down menu on the screen.

3. In the event that you're going to remove an author, you will then be prompted to either delete the content that the author

wrote or have it attributed to another writer.

This process is used to ensure that an old user can be removed and that the content that the person made can still be online if necessary. Be sure when managing the users on your WordPress page that you keep them under control. Check to see if you can trust in the people who are going to create content for your site so you'll have enough support as needed.

Chapter 10 – Important Tips

While you have learned plenty of things about WordPress in this guide, there are a few particular tips that deserve to be discussed. These are all ideal considerations to follow when aiming to make WordPress work to your liking.

Schedule Posts

You can always schedule posts on your page for the future if you have lots of content to post but you don't want to get it all out right away. You can schedule posts by choosing a particular date on the menu next to the Publish button.

The post can be scheduled based on the time and date that you want it to be up at. This can work for various individual posts and is perfect if you want to get a certain bit of content up and running at any time.

Be sure to click the Schedule button and not the Publish button in this case. This is to let WordPress know that a post will go up at a later time and not now.

Don't forget that the clock on the WordPress dashboard uses military time. If you're going to post something at nine in the evening then you should enter in 21:00 as the time that it will be posted at, for instance.

Adjust the URLs

You can always change the URL of whatever page or post you are adding. This is ideal for cases where you want to use particular keywords in the URL to make your page more visible from an SEO standpoint.

To do this, go to the URL listed near the title of your new post. Click on that URL and add new content based on what you want the name of the URL for that post to be.

Make sure you choose something that is relevant to your content. Also, do not use spaces when entering in the URL. Hyphens can be used to separate words or other bits of content.

Don't Rely Too Much On Spell Checkers

The integrated WordPress spell and grammar checker, as well as various more advanced plugins, can certainly warn you in the event that something is amiss with what you are writing. It lets you know when you're spelling things wrong among other points.

However, this does not mean that you should rely on it far too much. While it can be useful, you should still look through everything you are writing before posting it to ensure that you've got the content that you need.

The problem with some checkers is that they might miss lots of details. They might ignore sentences that go on for too long. They might not read overly verbose statements or cases where you're using the wrong tense or verb.

Be careful when writing anything on WordPress. Always use your best judgment and only use the grammar and spelling checkers are suggestions that might alert you to obvious issues.

Work With Videos and Social Media the Right Way

It is very easy to get different videos and social media files integrated into your WordPress post. You just have to enter in an appropriate URL from a site like YouTube, Twitter or Vimeo to make your content visible.

Don't try and align your URLs in some manner. While you might not see your video or other item at first, WordPress will read the information and generate an appropriate box to display a tweet, a YouTube video or whatever else you want to put into your post.

This part of integration should be easy to use. Don't try and make it more complicated than it has to be. Just work with the appropriate URL for whatever you want to post and it should work out just fine.

Always Keep WordPress Up to Date

Everything that you use when running WordPress needs to be fully up to date. The newest edition of WordPress has to be up and running so you can get access to everything it has to offer.

WordPress often releases new editions of the program that contain more features and support for more items and functions. More importantly, maintenance updates are also added to fix bugs in the system and to control any security threats that might show up.

Don't forget that many WordPress versions are named after famed jazz musicians. This is like how versions of the Android operating system are named after desserts. WordPress versions are named like this because the core developers of the program are also big fans of jazz music. Version 2.7 is known as John Coltrane while version 3.0 is Thelonious Monk, for instance. Version 4.5, which was introduced in April 2016, is the Coleman Hawkins edition. This has been updated a few times since it was released with new patches and bugs to fix up different problems in the system.

Don't forget to update your plugins. They too can be updated and improved upon regularly.

Back Up Your Site

You should always back up your site regularly to ensure that nothing wrong will come out of it. You should keep a backup of your WordPress database up and ready for use if your current version fails. This will allow you to back up the media files, posts and other pieces of information on your site.

You can back up your site as often as you want and with any outside backup program that you want to use. Be sure to prepare your backups often so it will be easier for you to keep your data under control without the risk of losing anything in particular.

Test Your Work On Many Devices

The last tip is to test your work on as many different devices as possible. While a great WordPress site will look beautiful, it must also load properly. It must be able to work on many computers, web browsers and operating systems.

Be sure to check on how well your site will load based on not only what you have added but also any URLs you are linking to. This is especially the case when you've got a video from another site that you are going to stream on your WordPress page.

Everything should be checked regularly to see that it is loading quickly enough. This is to keep people on many computers and operating systems from being frustrated with trying to load up your site.

More importantly, this makes it easier for your site to be listed on a search engine. Faster-loading sites are better for SEO purposes.

Conclusion

We hope that you have learned quite a bit about how to use WordPress through this guide. As you have learned here, WordPress is a great solution for your website development needs that is easy to use. It is amazingly versatile and can work with all sorts of users depending on your demands.

Make sure you refer to this guide regularly as you are creating your WordPress page. Check to see that you are drafting content in a responsible manner and that you are fully aware of what might make your content work out right.

Most importantly, make sure when creating a WordPress page that you are drafting content that is easy to follow. By using the points listed in this guide, you will see that using WordPress is easy to do and that you can quickly get different pieces of content up and running on WordPress without worrying about things being too complicated or tough.

Have fun with WordPress and make sure to take advantage of everything it has to offer. You will love the final result when you've created your own special page.

37386027R00037

Made in the USA
San Bernardino, CA
16 August 2016